The Flow System Guide

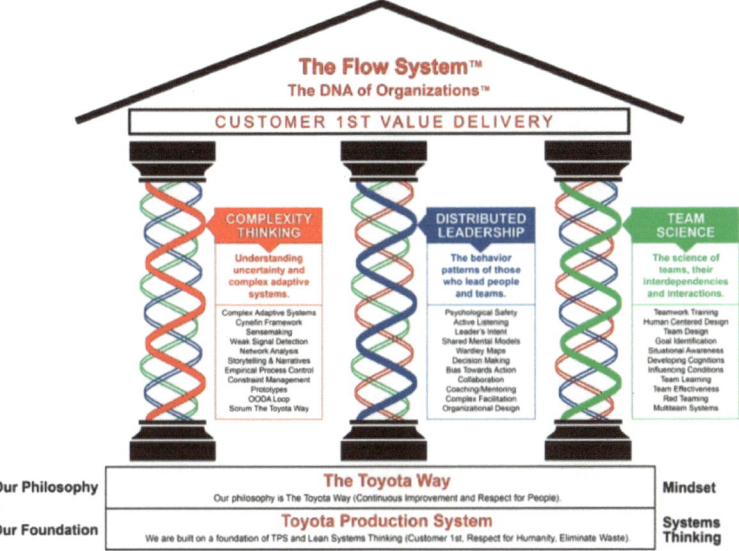

Written by:
John R. Turner, Ph.D.
Nigel Thurlow
Brian 'Ponch' Rivera

Version 1.0 (November 2019)

Copyright © 2020, Copyright John R. Turner Ph.D., Nigel Thurlow, and Brian Rivera. All right reserved. This book or parts thereof may not be reproduced in any form, stored in any retrieval system, or transmitted in any form by any means- spoken, written, photocopy, printed, electronic, mechanical, recording, or otherwise through any means not yet known or yet in use-without prior written permission of the authors, except for purposes of review.

Published by The Flow Consortium

ISBN: 9798622569449

Table of Contents

Table of Contents 3
The Purpose of The Flow System™ 5
Definition of The Flow System™ 7
A Brief History of The Flow System™ 9
Core Principles of The Flow System™ 12
1. Customer 1st 14
2. FLOW of Value 16
3. The Triple Helix of Flow™ 18
3a. Complexity Thinking 21
Complex Adaptive Systems 24
The Cynefin® Framework 25
Sensemaking 27
Weak Signal Detection.......................................28
Network Analysis..29
Storytelling and Narratives 29
Empirical Process Control 30
Constraint Management 31
Prototypes..32
The OODA Loop 32
Scrum the Toyota Way 33
3b. Distributed Leadership 35
Psychological Safety 38
Active Listening..38
Leader's Intent 39
Shared Mental Models 40

Wardley Maps	41
Decision Making	42
Bias Towards Action	43
Collaboration	43
Coaching	44
Complex Facilitation	44
Organizational Design	45
3c. Team Science	47
Teamwork Training	49
Human Centered Design	49
Team Design	50
Goal Identification	52
Situational Awareness	53
Developing Cognitions	53
Influencing Conditions	54
Team Learning	54
Team Effectiveness	55
Red Teaming	55
Multiteam Systems	56
TFS Theory	58
Applying TFS	61
References	64

The Purpose of The Flow System™

Achieving a state of flow occurs when organizations/institutions produce outcomes in which their constraints (e.g., structure, processes, environmental effects) are shaped in a way that enable employees to concentrate on their own interactions among one another and the customer. Flow ultimately results in employees concentrating on the act of doing rather than combatting or succumbing to organizational friction.

Many project management methods and agile frameworks concentrate on taskwork and the illusion of planning with no regard to how an organization is structured to support these activities. Organizations/institutions utilize teams but fall short in developing teamwork skills and fail to restructure leadership to maximize the benefits that can be obtained from the utilization of teams. These shortcomings introduce additional constraints and barriers that prevent organizations/institutions from achieving a state of flow.

The Flow System™ provides a re-imagined system for organizations to understand complexity, embrace teamwork, and autonomous team-based leadership structures.

Definition of The Flow System™

The Flow System™ enables business growth by eliminating non-value added activities by fostering an environment for innovation and the rapid delivery of value, and shortening the time to market.

The Flow System™ is a holistic FLOW based approach to delivering Customer 1st Value. It is built on a foundation of The Toyota Production System, also known as TPS and LEAN, plus a new triple helix structure known as the DNA of Organizations™.

The Flow System™ provides an understanding of different methods, patterns, practices, and techniques that enable organizations or institutions to achieve their desired outcomes.

A Brief History of The Flow System™

The Flow System™ has evolved from the emergence of product delivery in non-linear environments, also known as complex environments or complexity. It has expanded upon the work done between 1948 and 1975 on the Toyota Production System (TPS is also known as Lean), and the Toyota Way, first published in 2001 by Toyota. The Flow System™ is the evolution of lean thinking that we call flow thinking.

The Toyota Production System has become a model for organizations to achieve manufacturing excellence at the highest level of quality that is achievable. The Toyota Production System has as its primary focus the Customer. The Toyota Production System is built upon the pillars of *Jidoka* and *Just in Time*. Jidoka includes having the ability to stop a machine or process if and when a problem occurs. Just in Time includes the elimination of waste by removing non-value added activities.

The foundation for the Toyota Production System is *Standardization*, establishing repeatable and predictable processes, and *Kaizen*, the philosophy of continuous improvement. The Toyota Production System has become the reference system when approaching linear and repeatable manufacturing. However, it is limited when dealing with ambiguous problems, highly variable processes, non-linearity, and unpredictability, all features of complexity.

The Toyota Way 2001 clarifies the values and business methods that all employees should embrace. Represented as the *Guiding Principles* of Toyota, the Toyota Way is depicted by the pillars of *Continuous Improvement* and *Respect for People*.

Toyota is never completely satisfied with where they are and are continuously working to improve their practices by advancing new ideas and empowering its workforce. Toyota respects its employees, shareholders, and stakeholders, and believe talented individuals and good teamwork create their success. Fulfilling its role as the backbone of an organization, an organization's culture must evolve amid an ever-changing business environment.

The creators of The Flow System™ recognized that existing tools and frameworks could not holistically address complexity as organizations are not optimized to function in volatile and ambiguous environments. They also recognized that complexity thinking is different from lean thinking, and that new approaches and understanding are called for.

The creators of The Flow System™ acknowledge all the great minds that have created the thinking we follow today (too many to mention here) and have preserved the Toyota Production System and The Toyota Way as the inspiration and foundation of The Flow System™.

Core Principles of The Flow System™

The Flow System™ consists of 3 core principles.
1. Customer 1st.
2. The FLOW of value.
3. The Triple Helix of Flow™.
    a. Complexity Thinking
    b. Distributed Leadership
    c. Team Science

1. Customer 1st

Since 1946 Toyota Motor Corporation has always placed the Customer first. In May 1946, Shotaro Kamiya, the first President of Toyota Motor Sales Co., Ltd. Japan, was the first Toyota executive to publicly declare that "the primary focus must *always* be the customer."

That Customer 1st promise has been enshrined in The Toyota Production System and The Toyota Way ever since. Consideration of the customer's needs is foundational when determining the direction and strategy of the organization. The customer 1st promise produces three outcomes:

1. Highest Quality.
2. Lowest Cost.
3. Shortest Lead-Time.

The Flow System™ recognizes that this still holds today and that no organization or institution will ultimately succeed if they lose focus on the customer. The Flow System™ also highlights the components of *Respect for Humanity* and *Respect for People* as essential elements for ethically delivering on the Customer 1st promise.

Respect for humanity is a foundational component of TPS, and respect for people is a key pillar in The Toyota Way along with the philosophy of continuous improvement. At Toyota, respect for humanity is a matter of allying human energy with meaningful, effective operations by abolishing wasteful operations [Prof. Yasuhiro Monden, 1983]. A key approach is 'Monozukuri wa hitozukuri', translated as 'developing products through developing people'.

We understand that without the customer, we have no employees, no investors, no shareholders, and no investments for community development. It starts with the Customer 1st.

2. FLOW of Value

Once a customer exists, the focus then shifts to sustaining that customer. Maintaining a customer requires an organization that can configure itself to continue the flow of value to that customer.

Flow is an evolving concept with knowledge gained from multiple fields of study (e.g., anthropology, biology, ecology, physics, psychology, team science). As an evolving state, a system's configuration must evolve, adapt, and transform into new structures that support delivering seamless processes free of inhibiting constraints that are capable of operating in disruptive and complex environments.

Flow is a collective social motion in which individuals, or agents, learn to understand and react to their environment to obtain the goals of delivering value to the customer.

In The Flow System™, as the components of complexity thinking, distributed leadership, and team science become more and more interconnected over time flow becomes more seamless and natural. At this point, a *state of flow* is said to be achieved.

Creating a flow of value requires organizations to configure themselves in such a way to enable Customer 1st outcomes.

3. The Triple Helix of Flow™

The Triple Helix of Flow™ consists of 3 individual strands of organizational DNA; Complexity Thinking, Distributed Leadership, and Team Science. The DNA of Organizations™.

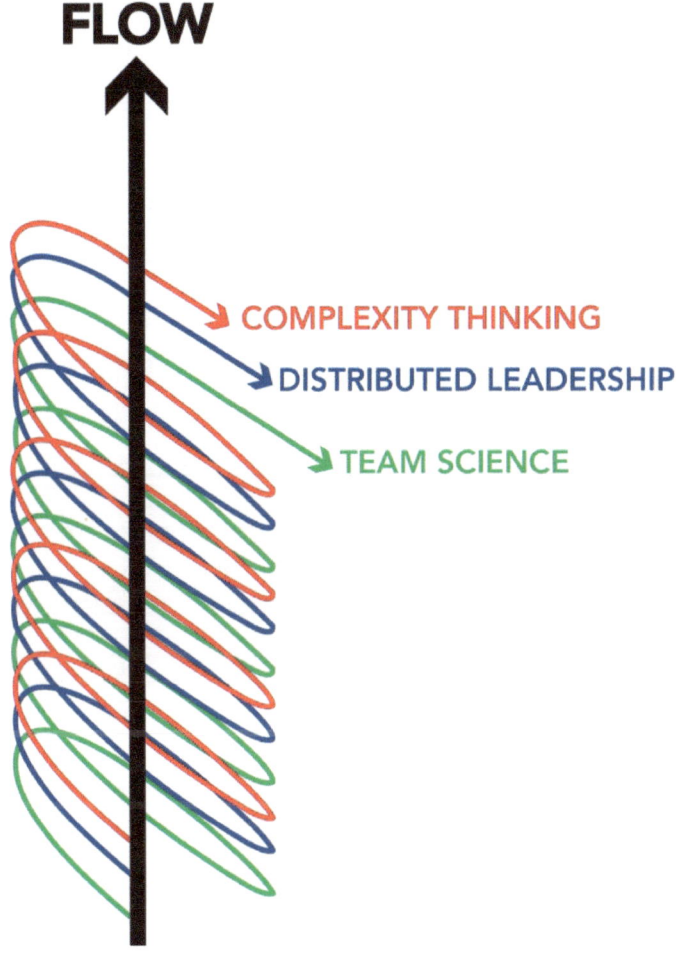

The Triple Helix of Flow™ relates to the interconnected nature of the three helixes (complexity thinking, distributed leadership, team science). The triple helix identifies the interactions between and among agents (e.g., people, machines, events) that emerge into new patterns, networks, and knowledge to advance an organization's ability to be more innovative, adaptive, and agile when operating in complex environments.

Implementing the Triple Helix of Flow™ will require a level of organizational transformation to take place. A change is necessary to assure that each of the three helixes is indeed truly interconnected, synchronized, and embedded in an organization's structure, allowing for seamless movement from ideation to value delivery to the customer.

Flow is achieved through the interactions of agents in a constraint-free environment when using the methods, techniques, and tools identified under each of the helixes in The Flow System™ – acknowledging that the needs of each organization/institution are different. These differences result in each organization/institution needing to implement various methods, techniques, and tools to achieve a state of flow for their purpose.

It is not the aim of The Flow System™ to utilize, practice, and master every method, technique, and tool listed. What is critical, however, is that each organization or institution finds the best methods, techniques, and tools from each of the three helixes to allow them to achieve their desired goals. Implementing new practices through the interconnection of the three helixes into one cohesive system delivers uninterrupted flow.

The concept of FLOW is an evolving process, as the components of complexity thinking, distributed leadership, and team science become more interconnected over time. Flow becomes even more seamless, natural, and unnoticed.

3a. Complexity Thinking

The first helix in the Triple Helix of Flow™ is complexity thinking.

Complexity thinking is a new form of thinking to aid in understanding uncertainty and complex adaptive systems. It is first essential to understand that not everything is predictable due to the unknown-unknowns that are present in complex environments. Complex environments involve multiple possible states, varying from location to location, and can change conditions rapidly in a short amount of time. It is the understanding of the variety in one's environment that is essential to complexity thinking. Once the variety in one's climate has been identified, complexity thinking can be applied.

Complexity thinking involves two primary steps:

> Step 1: Understanding the characteristics of complex systems.
> Step 2: Have a worldview or perspective that systems, entities, and events are complex adaptive systems.

Operating in complex environments is an exploratory process where the whole is not understood completely. Complexity thinking, in part, aids in being able to focus on what cannot be explained as opposed to focusing on what can be explained. Due to the ambiguity, uncertainty, and unknowns that are present in complexity, specific methods, techniques, and tools have been identified to help navigate these waters.

The methods, techniques, and tools for the helix of complexity thinking include:

- Complex Adaptive Systems
- The Cynefin® Framework
- Sensemaking
- Weak Signal Detection
- Network Analysis
- Storytelling and Narratives
- Empirical Process Control
- Constraint Management
- Prototypes
- The OODA Loop
- Scrum the Toyota Way.

Complex Adaptive Systems

Definition
Complex adaptive systems (CAS) are dynamic, open, and self-organizing systems with permeable constraints or boundaries that interact with feedback mechanisms to become adaptive. Complex adaptive systems are dynamic, continuously learn to adapt to external forces, and emerge to new states when necessary to meet unique environmental needs.

Explanation
Several social systems have been described as being a complex adaptive system. For example, complex adaptive systems can include entrepreneurship, governments, organizations, teams, and even societies.

Characteristics
Complex adaptive systems include the following characteristics:
- they are path-dependent,
- the systems have a history,
- they are non-linear,
- they include emergent outcomes,
- their processes are irreducible,
- they are adaptive,
- they operate between order and chaos, and
- they are self-organizing [1].

The Cynefin® Framework

Definition
The Cynefin® Framework, by David Snowden [2] [3], includes five distinct domains. The framework is used primarily to consider the dynamics of situations, decisions, perspectives, conflicts, and changes to come to a consensus for decision making under uncertainty.

These domains provide clarification as to what type of methods, tools, or techniques may be required when operating in each of them.

It enables executives to see things from new viewpoints, assimilate complex concepts, and address real-world problems and opportunities. Using the Cynefin® Framework can help executives sense which context they are in so that they can make better decisions and avoid issues that can arise when their current management style causes them to make mistakes.

Cynefin®, pronounced kuh-nev-in, is a Welsh word that signifies the multiple factors in our environment and our experiences that influence us in ways we can never understand.

Explanation
When dealing with complex problems, such as climate change, the problem is ill-defined, and the solution is unknown. The components that lead to the issues we are experiencing with climate change are also unknown. The methods, techniques, and tools used for problems in the complex domain are drastically different from those found in the simple domain.

The Cynefin® Framework enables us to categorize problems into domains that allow us to select the appropriate tools that can be used to address these problems. For example, in the clear or complicated domains, we may choose Lean tools, whereas, in the complex domain, we may need Sensemaking.

Characteristics
The domains of knowledge for the Cynefin® Framework include the clear, complicated, complex, chaotic, and disordered domains. It is a decision-making framework. As of late 2019, David Snowden has suggested changing the simple/obvious domain to clear.

Sensemaking

Definition

Sensemaking is a technique designed to aid our understanding of complex problems and conditions or environments. Sensemaking aids in developing stories around one's environment in which individuals and groups can begin developing shared mental models to understand the complex environment or problem better.

Explanation

In complex environments, stories and narratives aid in understanding the conditions of the environment/situation. During firefighting efforts, teams of firefighters continuously communicate their view of their surroundings to other team members, aiding in each team member's understanding of the current situation. These stories, from multiple team members, assist in the team's ability to make sense of their surroundings.

Characteristics

Sensemaking includes the following characteristics: "interaction and conversation (social), clearer frames of reference (identity), relevant past experiences (retrospect), neglected details in the current environment (cues), updating of impressions that have changed (ongoing), plausible stories of what could be happening (plausibility), and actions that clarify thinking (enactment)" [4]. Sensemaking is most effective when conducted in real-time.

Weak Signal Detection

Definition
Weak signal detection is a method which can detect the sign of future changes at an early stage and involves identifying opportunities and threats that exist in the environment. Weak signal detection is essential to identifying early signs of problems before they become unmanageable and is a method that can detect the sign of future changes at an early stage.

Weak signals are an advanced indicator of change, and they must be acknowledged. Sudden and unfamiliar changes in an organization can threaten any division of that organization. Unacknowledged changes could result in significant profit reversal or loss of new opportunities [5]. Continually searching and monitoring one's environment can provide early detection of threats that would have otherwise gone undetected.

Explanation
Being able to detect business threats before countermeasures are found to be ineffective is one form of weak signal detection. Weak signal detection is necessary for safety-critical environments. Tools and techniques must be put in place to detect these weak signals to ensure sustainability for an organization or institution. If management is receptive to weak signals, much can be done long before the threat becomes tangible and concrete.

Characteristics
Weak signal detection involves continuously scanning the environment using different perspectives (cross-disciplinary points of view) to identify any abnormal behaviors, signals, or events in the background, internal and external.

Network Analysis

Definition

Open systems, such as complex adaptive systems, can be viewed and analyzed as a network. Network analysis allows you to view the interactions, or linkages, between components, such as the interactions between teams, or between organizations. Network analysis can inform for developing practical ways to ensure a sufficient flow of information between systems and agents.

Explanation

Networks analysis has been used to analyze many different types of networks, such as culture, nature, brains, organisms, economies, and ecologies [6]. Network analysis has been used to identify key people in organizational units that hold essential information to the success of the organization. Understanding how these various networks communicate, share, and store information, and collaborate is necessary for effective organizational design.

Characteristics

Network analysis is flexible in that it can analyze dyads (e.g., person to person), nodes (e.g., leader, team, organization), and networks (e.g., leader to individuals, team to team). Network analysis views the relationships, links, or interactions between each set of dyads, nodes, and networks.

Storytelling and Narratives

Definition

Knowledge creation through people externalizing their sense of understanding, i.e., what does something or a particular event mean to them? Through these narratives (a spoken or written account of connected events), or stories, we can begin to form a more significant representation of what is occurring in complex environments.

Explanation
A Jury in the court system often makes decisions based on the stories and narratives they are exposed to during a trial. Jury members try to make sense of these stories in their deliberations. A jury's decision could be considered a synthesis of these stories or narratives. In business, collecting narratives and stories from employees can give a company or organization a sense of its current climate.

If we ask employees to write a news headline and an associated news report on a relevant topic or issue, we are then able to synthesize common themes and patterns that can inform future decision making, strategies, and planning.

Characteristics
Narratives are often expressed through artifacts, writing, recordings, language, metaphors, and stories.

Empirical Process Control

Definition
Science is a process that tests theories that explain or predict a phenomenon or problem. This empirical process includes many different methods and procedures that are valid, reliable, and rigorous – they have been tested and validated over time. Empirical processes are objective and attempt to remove subjectivity, human biases, from any decision-making outcomes. Experimentation is believed to be fundamental to our understanding of our environment, providing further clarification of the unknown or unobservable.

Explanation
Science provides a wealth of examples that show, not only how empirical processes advance new knowledge, but also how

findings from empirical research can challenge current beliefs, practices, and dogma. One derived example of this is PDCA (Plan, Do, Check, Act), an iterative four-step process to control and enable continuous improvement of processes and products.

Characteristics

Empirical processes vary from one discipline to the next requiring active engagement [7] of the following components: problem identification, defining the problem if possible, theorizing, measuring, observing, analyzing, interpreting, and reporting.

Constraint Management

Definition

Constraints are limitations or restrictions that affect the behaviors of agents. Constraints are self-derived and cognitively constructed. Realizing what constraints are in place is essential for any team or organization in complex environments. Managing to remove unnecessary constraints is necessary for an organization to function effectively. Constraints can be enabling or inhibiting.

Enabling constraints make it possible for agents to do something that would not be possible otherwise. Inhibiting constraints hinder agents in doing something or only allow them to do it in a certain way.

Explanation

To enable and optimize flow in an organization, we need to limit the number of inhibiting constraints while optimizing enabling constraints. An enabling constraint allows an agent to operate with autonomous decision making, but within boundaries that are defined to prevent undesirable outcomes. An enabling constraint is value added. Directed, mandated, or required by regulatory agencies often impose inhibiting constraints. An inhibiting constraint typically has no value-added benefits.

Characteristics
Storytelling, developing shared mental models, the sharing of narratives, and identification of weak signals are successful constraint management techniques.

Prototypes

Definition
A prototype is a representation, a physical model, or a formula of a complex problem. Through continuous testing and refinement, prototypes make part of a complex problem concrete, contributing to a better understanding of complexity.

Explanation
Rather than design a full model (automobile) for a new customer-base (autonomous-driving car), it is cheaper and more effective, to begin with identifying individual components to find what is desirable/acceptable to the customer, as opposed to building an entire car first.

Characteristics
Prototypes can take the form of an experiment, a model (computer or physical), or a formula (computational). A prototype must have some familiarity or relationship to the whole. A prototype can aid in understanding the whole by modeling the familiar (parts of what is known) to understand the unfamiliar (the unknowns) [8].

The OODA Loop

Definition
The observe-orient-decide-act (OODA) loop is a non-linear decision-making process, a guide for action. The OODA loop represents 40 years of work by Air Force Colonel John Boyd who

combined lessons from fighter aviation, strategy, science, early complexity thinking, and the Toyota Production System.

Explanation

The OODA loop is a decision-making process. It ensures all available relevant information is observable and trains an observer on how to orient herself for effective decision making. Once the right decisions are determined, it enables the rapid execution of those decisions. However, it is possible first to act, then observe and orient to the outcomes of the action, and this will inform future decision making.

The OODA loop favors implicit over explicit decision-making processes. It contains sensemaking (observation and orientation) loops to feature the separation of decisions from outcomes when assessing individual and organizational performance. The OODA loop is described as "an evolving, open-ended, far from equilibrium process of self-organization, emergence and natural selection" [9].

Characteristics

The OODA loop can begin at either stage in the loop and is dependent on the problem or situation at hand. The components of the OODA loop include observe, orient, decide, and act, and is an iterative cycle. The focal point of the OODA loop is orientation- those heuristics, cognitive biases, and established beliefs that determine how individuals and organizations observe, decide, and act.

Scrum the Toyota Way

Definition

A training program that is designed to aid employees and organizations to develop agility as an emergent outcome through problem identification and definition skills, customer profiles, teamwork skills, planning, and estimation skills, and to gain visualization techniques. It enables organizations to understand the boundaries between systems thinking approaches and complexity thinking strategies through the application of the Scrum framework as a behavioral pattern, as well as a range of tools and cognitive skills.

Explanation

Departments/divisions of organizations learn to operate more effectively as functional high performing teams through their training using the techniques from the Scrum the Toyota Way training.

Characteristics

Scrum the Toyota Way can be characterized by the implementation of, or refinement of, various tools, techniques, and concepts.

3b. Distributed Leadership

The concept of distributed leadership entails leadership that extends horizontally, vertically and every place in-between within an organization. Leadership begins with the individual, and the model of leadership becomes a collective construct.

Leadership is developed and practiced at the individual level with self-leadership and self-efficacy development techniques. Shared leadership becomes the model of leadership at the team level, with a functional leadership model acting as the oversight of the teams.

Functional leadership views the leader-team relationship as opposed to most leadership models that see the leader-follower dyad. Functional leadership, also called boundary spanners, operate in the boundaries between teams and between teams and multiteam systems. Their roles and responsibilities include providing resources, fostering interactions, coordination of activities, and alignment of goals, to name only a few. At the executive level or the C-suite, leadership can remain in its traditional hierarchical structure if desired.

Research has shown that many team-based structures and multiteam systems have functioned well using a hybrid style of leadership. A hybrid or blended leadership model is embedded in The Flow System™. This hybrid leadership model incorporates components of the following leadership theories that have been shown to work well with team-based organizational structures and for complex environments: strategic leadership, instrumental leadership, and global leadership.

The intention is not for every organization to implement all three leadership models at their executive level but to implement the components from each leadership theory that meets the needs of the organization in a way that best supports the team-based structures previously outlined. The needs of one organization will be different from another, and each organization needs to identify which characteristics and components of leadership are best for their organizational needs.

The distributed leadership helix of The Flow System™ provides a process that continually revives leaders throughout an organization, allowing the collective leadership to emerge within an organization that is capable of making bold and disruptive moves across an industry.

The methods, techniques, and tools for the distributed leadership helix include the following:

- Psychological Safety
- Active Listening
- Leader's Intent
- Shared Mental Models
- Bias Towards Action
- Collaboration
- Coaching/Mentoring
- Complex Facilitation
- Organizational Design

Psychological Safety

Definition
Psychologically safe environments are where team members or employees can freely express their opinions and ask questions without being ridiculed or reprimanded. The best descriptor is that team members and employees are free to be candid [10] as long as their views and criticisms remain professional. Psychological safety eliminates a culture of fear.

Explanation
In Toyota's Production System, employees can freely pull the Andon cord. The Andon cord consists of a pull cord that runs the length of the production line, or sometimes a button that workers can activate to stop the production and warn management in case of a significant issue or the potentiality of a problem.

Employees freely pull the Andon cord when they see a problem with no fear of being reprimanded or punished for stopping production. The Andon cord acts as a metaphor for a psychologically safe working environment where employees are free to question and probe to assure that the right decisions or actions are being taken. It also ensures the right people are taking those actions.

Characteristics
Psychological safety portrays the following features: a shared expectation, shared purpose, confidence in being heard, accepting failure, continuously learning [10].

Active Listening

Definition
Leadership involves listening as much as it consists of talking. Active listening is an essential leadership characteristic that can be

developed. It refers to a pattern of listening that keeps you engaged with the conversation positively. It is the process of listening attentively while someone else speaks, paraphrasing and reflecting what was said, withholding judgment, or giving advice.

Explanation

Leaders must listen to hear the problems that their followers are encountering. Interactions between leaders and followers, should not only take the direction of the leader, but a leader must interact with their followers to understand their problems, and must also talk with them to instill purpose and meaning in their work.

The Andon cord is again a great example where active listening takes place. Activation of an Andon cord initiates a series of interactions between the leader/supervisor and the employee. These interactions involve equal parts of listening and talking from both parties to understand and resolve the problem.

Characteristics

Active listening aids leaders in their sensemaking processes through the functions of listening and talking, building trust, establishing rapport, demonstrating concern, asking a specific question, and using brief affirmations. Active listening aids one's cognitive processes to understand better others' needs rather than focus on one's ideas and preconceived notions.

Leader's Intent

Definition

Leader's intent focuses on the desired outcome as opposed to a specific result. Through the understanding of the leader's intent and the desired outcome, individuals and teams are free to operate as necessary as long as they keep in mind the desired result. There is no one correct way to achieve an outcome, and through the model presented as the leader's intent, individuals and teams are free to find their way.

Explanation
Also associated with the commander's intent, military squads have a general idea of the overall objective. However, when engaged, there are too many unknowns to follow a detailed plan. Squadrons are free to alter their course of action as required to achieve their end goal.

Characteristics
The characteristics of the leader's intent include planning, mission analysis, course of action development/analysis/comparison/approval, followed by a final review. A leader's intent is the personal expression of the purpose of the outcomes desired. It must be clear, concise, and easily understood. It may also include how the leadership envisions achieving a decision, as well as the end statement or conditions that accomplish the purpose.

Shared Mental Models

Definition
A shared mental model is the development of a collective understanding of, perception of, or knowledge about, a situation or process shared among team members.

Explanation
When team members begin planned work in which each team member has a different understanding of the team's objective, this would be indicative of a team that has not developed a shared mental model. Team members must be able to discuss all tasks and goals so that each member has a similar and accurate understanding. Effective planning and briefing techniques must be in place to aid in developing shared mental models.

Characteristics
This collective understanding involves members having a shared understanding of the problem, definitions, processes, goals, and resources.

Wardley Maps

Definition
Visualization techniques are critical to understanding complexity. Wardley maps are representations of an organization's landscape and structure of a business or service, mapping the components to serve the customer needs. It can be utilized to highlight patterns that are unobservable, increasing one's situation awareness.

Wardley maps are named after Simon Wardley who claims to have created them in 2005

Explanation
A Wardley map can be drawn to highlight the processes for developing a product. The map identifies the evolution (time-based) of each process (on the x-axis) involved in developing the product. The processes that are visible to the customer are positioned high on the y-axis, the processes that are essentially non-visible to the customer are positioned low on the y-axis.

When mapped out, the organization can see which processes include non-value added activities to the customer and which ones maximize value to the customer. This realization can allow organizations to refocus their processes to meet the customer's needs better.

Characteristics
Wardley maps include the following elements: visualization, context-specific, the position of components, and movement that

incorporates four types along the y-axis; activities (high visibility), practices, data, and knowledge (low visibility) [11].

Decision Making

Definition
Teams that are cross-functional and diverse are capable of addressing more complex problems than any one person can on their own. Developing team decision-making skills is critical before teams are capable of functioning autonomously, allowing organizations with the capability to be more adaptive.

Explanation
A team is more able to identify weak signals from a variety of sources in real-time, providing team members with several alternatives to choose from when making a decision. Decisions are no longer attributable to any single individual as they belong to the collective, the team. Team decision-making processes provide a more comprehensive range of options to choose from, one that includes more diversity and inclusion, compared to what individuals could provide.

Characteristics
Multiple individuals collaborating, analyze problems or situations, consider and evaluate alternative courses of action, and select from among the alternatives a solution or solutions. Team decision making involves an agreement of the problem, resources (information, knowledge, technology), and the requisite knowledge, skills, and abilities within the team to address the issue.

Bias Towards Action

Definition
A leadership technique that empowers both leaders and teams to make their own decisions in times of uncertainty.

Explanation
Bias towards action focuses on acting on ideas and begin to put changes in motion, rather than to concentrate on discussing potential ideas and changes. The leader (coach) and team make decisions together to decide their course of action to eliminate their competition (external forces). Companies need to focus on making progress rather than endlessly pursuing perfection.

Characteristics
Leaders and teams act autonomously and are free to self-organize and adapt. Reduction of distractions. Make smaller decisions. Stop overthinking. Focus on purposeful action.

Collaboration

Definition
To work jointly with others or together, especially in an intellectual endeavor. Collaboration is the process of two or more people, or organizations, working together to complete a task or to achieve a goal or an outcome.

Explanation
Teams are collaborations, but so are small groups and departments, classrooms, training sessions, social gatherings, and local politics. Structured methods of collaboration encourage introspection of behavior and communication. Such techniques aim to increase the success of collaboratives as they engage in complex problem-solving. Collaboration has become expected within organizations

and involves members who participate in knowledge creation and dissemination.

Characteristics
Collaboration involves effective communication, active listening, team planning, the ability to innovate, the sharing of knowledge, a diverse skill set, access to resources, clear expectations, and a shared goal.

Coaching

Definition
Coaching is a role that is designed to assist employees and team members in increasing their capacity, allowing them to manage their processes, to develop their full potential, and to become independent.

Explanation
A coach helps to train and educate team members on how to succeed together as a single unit. They are responsible for training team members by analyzing their performance, instructing in relevant skills, and by providing encouragement, mentorship, and leadership. A coach helps others to learn.

Characteristics
Coaching can be an external person, but it can also be an individual team member as a coach as well. Coaching involves developing skills and techniques, motivating team members, instilling meaning and clarity to work, providing feedback with recommendations for improvement, help coordinate activities and resources, and aim to have team members become self-leading and independent.

Complex Facilitation

Definition
Complex facilitation is a technique used to identify unknowns using cognitively diverse groups who affected by the complex problem. This facilitation technique removes the facilitator from the process and operates in a self-organizing fashion. This form of facilitation is counterintuitive and requires some unlearning methods.

Explanation
An example of complex facilitation would be an unconference session. An unconference session is where people meet in a conference room at their convenience and voice issues or concerns that they wish to discuss. As time goes on, the unconference provides a group of clusters that reflect the concerns of the participants.

Characteristics
Traditional facilitation requires that you keep a group on track towards a stated goal, doing your utmost to remove any barriers in the process and content. Complex facilitation involves the removal of an official facilitator, removal of all power or hierarchical titles, requires disruptions and can feel chaotic at times.

Organizational Design

Definition
Organizational design is a step-by-step methodology that identifies dysfunctional aspects of workflow, procedures, structures, and systems, realigning them to fit current business realities/goals and further developing plans to implement new changes. It is a process for shaping the way organizations are structured and run.

Explanation
Organized by hierarchical structures, the more complicated an organization's structure, the more inhibiting constraints there are

preventing an organization from delivering value to the customer. According to Conway's law [12], an organization's structure follows its lines of communication. In times of ambiguity, complexity, and disruption, organizations need to be designed using flatter structures, they need to become more adaptive, and they need to be able to support the team-based structures that they have recently built.

Characteristics

An organization's design should be representative of the individual workers, the teams, and multiteam systems with leadership roles that support each of these components. An organizational design needs to account for optimizing value-added activities, facilitating the flow of value to a customer. It serves the value stream, not the organization.

3c. Team Science

The field of team science is a discipline that studies all things related to teams and small groups in the workplace (e.g., interpersonal conflict, in-group and out-group dynamics, team psychological safety, team effectiveness).

Team science recognizes that teams are dynamic, cross-disciplinary, multidimensional, and complex adaptive systems. The helix of team science in The Flow System™ utilizes the team sciences to maximize the benefits of using team-based structures to address complex and disruptive environments.

The methods, techniques, and tools identified for the helix of team science include the following:

- Teamwork Training
- Human Centered Design
- Team Design
- Goal Identification
- Situational Awareness
- Developing Cognitions
- Influencing Conditions
- Team Learning
- Team Effectiveness
- Red Teaming
- Multiteam Systems

Teamwork Training

Definition
Team training is training in which teams are used to increase individual procedural knowledge and proficiency in doing a job (taskwork), along with developing interpersonal skills (teamwork) to function as a cohesive unit or team (performance). Teamwork training focuses on the team as a unit rather than concentrating on any single team member.

Explanation
Research has shown that teams with teamwork training perform better than teams with no training. Teams must be trained in teamwork skills before they can become effective teams. Teamwork skill development is the one key ingredient that separates mediocre performing teams (no teamwork skill training) with high performing teams (those with teamwork skill training). You cannot achieve high performing teams without first developing teamwork skills.

Characteristics
Teamwork training must:
- identify the requisite skills for the contextual setting,
- focus on learning the requisite teamwork skills,
- include training for all team members together,
- include briefing and debriefing activities,
- be done in real-time, and
- be evaluated for effectiveness.

Human Centered Design

Definition
Human centered design is a process that involves participation from all stakeholders (e.g., community members, customers, designers, employees, manufacturers, suppliers) during the design

stages. It includes the human element in the design of a new product and the solution to the problem.

Explanation
The very people who are affected by an issue are recruited to become involved in the design process to resolve the problem. Stakeholders can also become part of the design team. Human centered design utilizes participative involvement to help drive the design process to resolution, as opposed to focusing solely on documenting the problem.

Characteristics
One key component of human centered design is that the focus is on content as opposed to function, concentrating more on how a product fits a particular environment rather than on how it can function. Other characteristics include empathy, observation, collaboration, contextual framing, learning, visualization, and quick prototyping.

Team Design

Definition
Team design is the way teams are composed, assuring that the team has the requisite knowledge, skills, and abilities to complete the team's tasks.

Explanation
Effective team design is essential to the efficient delivery or completion of taskwork. It is also vital to enable effective teamwork. If a team is too large or too small or lacks the requisite skills and knowledge, it will become ineffective. If the team lacks essential teamwork skills (e.g., interpersonal and conflict management skills, motivation skills), it will also perform ineffectively. Team design or team composition is critical to a team's success.

Characteristics

Team composition characteristics include team member knowledge, skills, attitudes, and abilities; the team's diversity of knowledge and experiences; and team member demographics and cultural mix. A team should be large enough to accomplish its goals and objectives, but small enough to enable rapid decision making and execution activities.

Goal Identification

Definition

Goal identification is the desired outcome expected over a specific period. Goals occur at different levels of analysis, proximal goals are specific to individual teams, and distal goals connect proximal goals to broader organizational outcomes.

Explanation

Teams that focus solely on their own team's goals are dismissive of the overall organizational purpose, further separating the team from others with the potential of disrupting organizational outcomes.

Individual teams have their specific goals (proximal goals) that guide them toward goal accomplishment and must be associated with the overarching organizational goals (distal goals). Team goals must be in alignment with organizational goals, and all team members must be aware of both sets of goals and their connections. Both proximal and distal goals must be defined where multiple teams collaborate.

Characteristics

Team goals must be well defined, have measurable outcomes, and linked to an organization's overarching purpose. All members must know how each is related to one another.

Situational Awareness

Definition
The perception and comprehension that one has of their environmental elements, taking into account their knowledge that dictates how one will react to an event.

Explanation
The ability to recognize the threats, risks, and opportunities in real-time and to make rapid decisions on how to react.

Characteristics
Characteristics of situational awareness include one's ability to detect weak signals, to synthesize information, and to create new knowledge.

Developing Cognitions

Definition
At the individual level, developing cognitions involves the development of knowledge, skills, problem solving, and dispositions, which help individuals think about and understand the world around them.

Shared cognition occurs at the team level, where team members develop a level of shared-ness. Each team member needs to know who has what knowledge, skills, and experiences before performing the team's tasks.

Explanation
Team members must develop a shared understanding of their goals and be mindful of the team's knowledge and capabilities. Team members must also share information to improve the team's level of shared-ness and must be able to learn as a unit, adapting to changes as the team's cognition evolves.

Characteristics
Cognitions include all conscious and unconscious processes by which knowledge is accumulated, such as perceiving, recognizing, conceiving, and reasoning.

Influencing Conditions

Definition
Conditions in which team members have little to no control over are called influencing conditions.

Explanation
New team members have little to no control over the composition of the team they are assigned. New team members must adapt to the team, given its existing composition. Team influencing conditions support a team's core processes (cooperation, conflict, coordination, communication, coaching, cognition, cohesion, collective efficacy, and collective identity) [13].

Characteristics
Influencing conditions include a team's context, composition, culture, and diversity.

Team Learning

Definition
Team learning is a shared outcome of team member interactions.

Explanation
As team members interact with one another, they share new information that leads to the whole team learning. Teams that are unwilling to share information with other team members, such as teams that have low levels of psychological safety, are unable to learn and adapt as a cohesive unit.

Characteristics
Characteristics of team learning include dialogue and discussion, amplifying constructive conflict, dampening destructive conflict, and knowledge sharing, continuous reflection, and communication of actions.

Team Effectiveness

Definition
Team effectiveness is the point in which team processes are aligned with task demands and are considered optimized to produce the desired outcome.

Explanation
Effective teams have developed the capability to look inwards as well as outward. When looking at effective teams (high performing teams), they continually evaluate the experiences of each team member as well as identifying how well they achieved their goals. Without evaluating team member issues, relationship conflicts are left unchecked and begin to disrupt the team's effectiveness.

Characteristics
Team effectiveness relates to a team's outcome (performance) as well as the interactions (teamwork) and processes (teamwork and taskwork) used to produce a result. Team performance focuses on the team's output (e.g., quantity, quality), regardless of the teamwork or taskwork processes to get to that output. Team effectiveness is the focus of teamwork training.

Red Teaming

Definition
Red teaming is a cognitive approach designed to develop new pathways to better decision making within teams.

Explanation

Red Teaming rigorously challenges plans, policies, systems, or assumptions by adopting an adversarial approach. Red teaming utilizes a set of tools and techniques designed to mitigate cognitive bias, enhance critical thinking skills, create self-awareness, and improve empathy.

The utilization of a red team, an example of one of the tools within Red Teaming, usually consists of impartial observers tasked with challenging a plan and help identify gaps and threats to create countermeasures before implementation takes place.

Characteristics

Red Teaming techniques include challenging explicit and implicit assumptions, exposing hidden information, developing alternatives to uncover unseen biases. Red Teaming methods include critical analysis of the team's processes, requiring teams to have already developed a high level of psychological safety, and to have developed strong teamwork skills.

Multiteam Systems

Definition

Multiteam systems (MTS) are defined as two or more teams working toward a common superordinate goal (distal goal or MTS goal). Multiteam systems are structured so that each team has its own set of goals (proximal goals) and has at least one shared goal with the MTS (distal goal).

Explanation

An MTS structure provides the ability to coordinate activities between multiple teams that function collectively toward achieving a shared goal. The compositional attributes of an MTS involve multiple teams that are designed to work together and coordinate activities to meet the distal goal of the MTS and the organization.

Individual teams operate autonomously and design their proximal goals while also being connected to the overall MTS goals. Leadership structures need to be capable of managing the boundaries around the teams within the MTS; this is where distributed leadership becomes necessary.

The key to success of any organization operating at scale is to have an effective MTS design that functions in its contextual setting with appropriate leadership roles to facilitate and guide it.

Characteristics

Multiteam systems exhibit input (sharing across teams), process (interactions between teams), and outcome (outcomes related to MTS goals) interdependence. Multiteam systems are also composed of three attributes; compositional, linkage, and developmental.

TFS Theory

A theory provides an explanation or prediction of a phenomenon or problem. Some of the best theories are those that utilize knowledge gained from both research and practice. Here, theories that cross the theory-to-practice divide end up being more practical and pragmatic. The Flow System™ is such a theory; it draws upon empirically derived knowledge and from those who have worked in the field as a practitioner/consultant with years of experience. The Flow System™ also has the additional benefit of being able to draw upon the knowledge and skills gained from the U.S. military armed forces as one of the co-creators came from the U.S. Navy.

The phenomenon that is addressed by The Flow System™ is one that many organizations are dealing with today. How can organizations maximize the value delivered to the customer in times of complexity? From our experiences, and from what has been identified by research, organizations are having difficulty adjusting from their normal modes of operating to become more adaptive to ambiguous, disruptive, global, and complex environments.

In many instances, organizations fail to meet these challenges due to their inability to:
a) identify complexity and not knowing how to function in complex environments (complexity thinking),
b) have inadequate organizational and leadership structures (distributed leadership), and
c) have ill-defined teamwork skills and team-structures (team science).

The Flow System™ is a theoretical model designed to influence practice. The integration of the three helixes highlighted in The Flow System™ presents a new way of framing the phenomenon. This integration of the three helixes (complexity thinking, distributed leadership, team science), represents the concept of the Triple Helix of Flow™ . The helixes and the requirement of them needing to be interconnected were derived from both evidence-based research and practice. Ultimately, it was the intention of the creators of The Flow System™ to present a pragmatic model showing how we have conceptualized Flow, the ability to become more adaptive in the world of complexity to deliver value to the customer.

As with all theories, there are stages of testing and modification that are necessary across different industries and organizational settings. This testing and modification process helps to capture the theory's ability to represent the real-world phenomenon that it claims to portray. Testing will also provide further evidence of which methods, techniques, and tools work for different organizations and industries. Once The Flow System™ has been exposed to several tests, we will then be able to be more specific in identifying which methods, tools, and techniques are applicable for different contextual settings and organizations.

As with any research endeavor, theory testing becomes an essential iterative process toward the development of a more pragmatic theory that has utility across all types of industries and organizations. The introduction of The Flow System™ is only the beginning of this long journey and is considered a constant work-in-progress.

Applying TFS

The Flow System™ is not, nor should it be, viewed as a prescriptive model or framework. The essential realization in The Flow System™ is that the three helixes must be interconnected into one holistic unit at every level of an organization before reaching a state of flow. How one gets to this state of flow, however, will be different for each organization, large and small.

The methods, techniques, and tools presented in each of the three helixes are only provided as options for organizations/institutions to try to utilize. While some of these methods may work well for one type or size of an organization/institution, others may work better for different organizations/institutions. The methods, techniques, and tools presented in each of the three helixes are contextual and primarily aimed at addressing complex problems and environments. These are different than current methods, techniques, and tools used today that mainly deal with simple and complicated problems.

Each organization/institution deals with different types of problems at various levels of complexity. The mechanisms they use to manage complex environments will most likely be different than those used by other organizations. The Flow System™ presents several tools for organizations/institutions to experiment with for them to find out which ones work best for their contextual setting. The key is for organizations/institutions to experiment with the various mechanisms in each of the three helixes until they find which methods, techniques, or tools work best for them. The result is for each organization/institution to be able to utilize a few of the methods, techniques, or tools presented from each of the three helixes for them to achieve flow.

The act of experimentation is essential for organizations/institutions to survive in complex environments. The Flow System™ acts as a guide for organizations/institutions to focus on during these experimentations.

References

1. Turner, J.R. and R. Baker, *Complexity theory: An overview with potential applications for the social sciences.* Systems, 2019. **7**(4): p. 23.
2. Kurtz, C.F. and D.J. Snowden, *The new dynamics of strategy: Sense-making in a complex and complicated world.* IBM Systems Journal, 2003. **42**: p. 462-483.
3. Snowden, D.J. and M.E. Boone, *A leader's framework for decision making.* Harvard Business Review, 2007. **85**(11): p. 68-76.
4. Weick, K.E., *Making sense of the organization: The impermanent organization.* Vol. 2. 2009, West Sussex, UK: John Wiley & Sons.
5. Ansoff, I.H., *Managing strategic surprise by response to weak signals.* California Management Review, 1975. **18**(2): p. 21-33.
6. Borgatti, S.G., M.G. Everett, and J.C. Johnson, *Analyzing social networks.* 2nd ed. 2018, Thousand Oaks, CA: SAGE.
7. Parsons, K., *It started with Copernicus: Vital questions about science.* 2014, Amherst, NY: Prometheus Books. 429.
8. Godfrey-Smith, P., *Theory and reality: An introduction to the philosophy of science.* 2003, Chicago, IL: University of Chicago Press.
9. Boyd, J. *The essence of winning and losing.* June 28, 1995; Available from: https://fasttransients.files.wordpress.com/2010/03/essence_of_winning_losing.pdf.
10. Edmondson, A.C., *the fearless organization: Creating psychological safety in the workplace for learning, innovation, and growth.* 2019, Hoboken, NJ: Wiley.
11. Wardley, S., *Finding a path*, in *Medium*. August 10, 2016, Medium: medium.com.
12. Conway, M.E., *How do committees invent?* Datamation, 1968. **14**(5): p. 28-31.

13. Dihn, J.V. and E. Salas, *Factors that influecne teamwork*, in *The Wiley Blackwell handbook of the psychology of team working and collaborative processes*, E. Salas, R. Rico, and J. Passmore, Editors. 2017, John Wiley & Sons: Malsen, MA. p. 15-41.

About the Authors

John R. Turner, Ph.D.

Dr. Turner is an assistant professor at the University of North Texas in the College of Information. He currently serves as the Editor–in–Chief for the Performance Improvement Quarterly (PIQ) journal. His research interests are in team science, team cognition, leadership, performance improvement, knowledge management, theory building, complexity theory, multilevel model development, and analysis techniques.

Dr. Turner is the co-creator of The Flow System and co-author of The Flow System Guide (https://flowguides.org/index.php). His website titled Team Science: Research, Technology, and Methods can be found at science-teams.com.

Dr. Turner's publications can be found in the following research journals: *Advances in Developing Human Resources*; *European Journal of Training & Development*; *Human Resource Development Review*; *International Journal of Technology, Knowledge, & Society*; *Journal of Information and Knowledge Management*; *Journal of Knowledge Management*; *Journal of Manufacturing Technology Management*; *New Horizons in Adult Education and Human Resource Development*; *Performance Improvement*; *Performance Improvement Quarterly*; and *Systems*.
ORCID: 0000-0003-0252-1531
ResearcherID: D-1633-2016

Nigel Thurlow

Nigel Thurlow has an extensive background in executive leadership across a diverse range of industry, including 15 years in various roles in Toyota companies globally.

He is the co-creator of The Flow System and co-author of The Flow System Guide (https://flowguides.org/index.php).

As the former Chief of Agile at Toyota Connected, he created 'Scrum The Toyota Way', an award winning and internationally recognized best in class training course, combining tools and concepts from the Toyota Production System, The Toyota Way, Lean, Agile and Scrum. This class has been recognized by multiple certification bodies. It was the recipient of a World Agility Forum award in 2018.

Nigel is recognized as an international expert in Toyota approaches as well as Lean, Agile, and Complexity concepts and has published peer reviewed white papers and journal publications on team science, and is a researcher currently working with a group of international scientists on leading edge research into where systems thinking and complexity thinking intersect. Nigel regularly speaks as an International Keynote at global events, many recordings of which are available online, and also acts as an advisor on several boards at the University of North Texas and was recently featured in an article by Forbes.

He also led the successful transformation at 3M Healthcare Information Systems and has taught and coached in notable companies such as GE, Bose, 3M, TJX, Microsoft, MA State Gov, and MIT. He was one of the earliest contributors to Scrum at Scale.

Brian Rivera

Brian 'Ponch' Rivera is a former F-14 TOPGUN pilot and political-military affairs expert. He is passionate about applying leadership and teamwork lessons he learned in the cockpit and from his experiences at the operational and strategic level of multi-domain (air, sea, land, space, and cyberspace) operations to organizational leaders who are interested in learning how to survive and thrive on their own terms.

He returned to active duty in 2018 to engage with industry and academia to identify industry 'Best Practices' behind changing culture, building high-performing teams, and capturing leading indicators.

As an Agile coach and consultant, Brian also speaks at Agile and Scrum conferences around the globe on topics ranging from human factors, high-reliability theory, the Cynefin framework, the OODA loop, red teaming techniques, and other components now found in The Flow System ™.

www.ingramcontent.com/pod-product-compliance
Lightning Source LLC
Chambersburg PA
CBHW041948240526
45473CB00036B/2540